# 01

## WHAT'S THE DIFFERENCE BETWEEN A LAWYER AND A HERD OF BUFFALO?

The lawyer charges more.

# 02

## A PAIR OF LAWYERS ENTERED A DINER AND ORDERED TWO BEVERAGES.

Afterward, they pulled out sandwiches from their briefcases and began eating. The concerned proprietor approached them and stated, "You're not allowed to consume your own sandwiches in this establishment!" The lawyers glanced at each other, nonchalantly shrugged, and proceeded to swap their sandwiches.

# KNOCK, KNOCK.

Who's there?
Will.
Will who?
Will you please stop objecting to everything I say?

# 04

## ONE EVENING, A LAWYER WAS WORKING LATE AT HIS OFFICE WHEN SUDDENLY SATAN APPEARED BEFORE HIM.

The Devil proposed to the lawyer, "I have an offer for you. From now on, you'll win every case you handle. Your clients will love you, your peers will be in awe of you, and you'll make an outrageous amount of money. In return, I want your soul, your wife's soul, your children's souls, the souls of your parents, grandparents, and in-laws, as well as the souls of all your friends and law partners."

The lawyer pondered over the proposal for a moment and then inquired, "Alright, but what's the downside?"

# 05

## WHY DON'T LAWYERS TRUST STAIRS?

They're always up to something.

# 06

## WHAT'S THE DIFFERENCE BETWEEN A LAWYER AND A LIAR?

The pronunciation.

# 07

## WHY DO THEY BURY LAWYERS 12 FEET DEEP?

Because deep down, they're really good people.

# 08

## WHY ARE LAWYERS LIKE MOVIE DIRECTORS?

They're always looking for a new angle.

# 09

# WHAT DO LAWYERS AND CHAMELEONS HAVE IN COMMON?

They can both change their colors to fit their surroundings.

# 10

## HOW MANY LAWYERS DOES IT TAKE TO CHANGE A LIGHTBULB?

It only takes one, but they'll bill you for three.

# 11

## A LAWYER WAS OBSESSED WITH FINDING THE PERFECT BRIEFCASE.

He spent years visiting every store he could find, searching online, and even traveling to other countries. One day, he finally found it - the perfect briefcase! He excitedly purchased it and brought it back to his office. As he proudly showed it off to his colleagues, one of them asked, "That's great, but what's so special about it?" The lawyer replied, "Well, it's like me - it has lots of pockets and always manages to stay closed!"

# 12

## WHY DID THE BLONDE LAWYER BRING A LADDER TO COURT?

She wanted to reach a higher settlement.

# 13

## DOCTOR, DOCTOR, MY LAWYER HAS A BAD CASE OF THE HICCUPS!

Just tell him he's about to lose a case, that should scare them away!

## 14

## I TOLD MY LAWYER I COULDN'T AFFORD HIS FEES

So he offered me a discounted rate - now he only charges an arm.

# 15

## I ONCE KNEW A LAWYER WHO WAS SO GOOD

He could convince a jury that the Earth was flat.

# 16

## THERE ONCE WAS A LAWYER NAMED DWIGHT

Who'd argue and fuss, day and night
His clients all cheered
When the verdicts were cleared
And he'd toast to his wins with delight

# 17

## I HIRED A LAWYER WHO CLAIMED TO BE A FORMER MAGICIAN.

I should've known better when he made my entire savings disappear.

# 18

## A LAWYER WALKS INTO A BAR AND ORDERS A MARTINI.

The bartender hands it to him and says, "Here's a little something to help you pass the bar."

# 19

## HOW MANY LAWYERS DOES IT TAKE TO SCREW IN A LIGHTBULB?

None, they'd rather keep their clients in the dark.

# 20

## WHY DO LAWYERS MAKE TERRIBLE DETECTIVES?

They're always trying to prove someone guilty.

# 21

## WHAT DO YOU CALL A LAWYER WITH A COOKING SHOW?

A sue chef.

# 22

## WHAT DO LAWYERS AND A BOX OF CHOCOLATES HAVE IN COMMON?

You never know what you're going to get, but it's probably going to be expensive.

# 23

## A MOTHER AND HER SON STROLLED THROUGH A GRAVEYARD WHEN THEY CAME ACROSS A TOMBSTONE THAT READ

"Resting here is an honest man and a good lawyer." The young boy studied the inscription, turned to his mother, and inquired, "Mom, why did they bury two people in the same grave?"

# 24

## AFTER YEARS OF HARD WORK, ANGIE TOOK HER FIRST VACATION ON A LUXURY CRUISE SHIP.

While sitting in a deck chair, she recognized a former school classmate, a long-lost friend from her old hometown. She crossed the deck and shook hands with her friend and said: "Hello, Angela. I haven't seen you in years. What are you doing these days?" "I'm a lawyer," whispered Angela. "But don't tell my mother. She still thinks I'm a prostitute."

# 25

## A MAN WALKED INTO A BAR WITH HIS ALLIGATOR AND ASKED THE BARTENDER

"Do you serve lawyers here?" "Sure do," replied the bartender. "Good," said the man. "Give me a beer, and I'll have a lawyer for my 'gator".

# 26

## A MAN, CONDEMNED TO HELL FOR HIS SINS

Was being escorted to his eternal punishment. As they passed a room, he noticed a lawyer engaged in a deep conversation with a stunning woman. "That's unfair," he grumbled. "I have to suffer forever, while that attorney enjoys time with such an attractive woman." Poking the man with his pitchfork, the demon retorted, "Who are you to question her punishment?"

## 27

**DID YOU HEAR ABOUT THE INDIVIDUAL WHO SUED AN AIRLINE AFTER THEY MISPLACED HIS LUGGAGE?**

Unfortunately, he couldn't win his case.

# 28

# ARGUING WITH AN ATTORNEY IS LIKE MUD-WRESTLING A PIG...

At some point, you realize they're actually enjoying it!

## 29

**DID YOU HEAR ABOUT THE LAWYER WHO TRIPPED OVER A STACK OF LEGAL DOCUMENTS AND FELL INTO A GIANT INKWELL?**

They were charged with practicing law in a black-and-white manner!

# 30

## KNOCK, KNOCK.

Who's there?

Justin.

Justin who?

Justin time for the trial, I found a lawyer!

# 31

## MY LAWYER IS SO GOOD AT NEGOTIATING

He could settle an argument between cats and dogs.

# 32

## WHAT DO YOU GET WHEN YOU CROSS A LAWYER WITH A COMPUTER?

A lot of well-documented arguments.

# 33

## HOW MANY LAWYERS DOES IT TAKE TO CHANGE A LIGHTBULB?

Just one, but they'll bill you for the research, the bulb, and the installation.

# 34

## WHY DID THE LAWYER JOIN THE ORCHESTRA?

He wanted to learn how to pull strings.

# 35

## A LAWYER WAS ONCE CALLED TO DEFEND A MAN ACCUSED OF STEALING A MASSIVE WHEEL OF CHEESE.

The evidence was stacked against his client, but the lawyer confidently approached the judge and said, "Your Honor, the prosecution's case is full of holes. It simply doesn't stand up to scrutiny." The judge replied, "Counselor, are you trying to make a Swiss cheese analogy?" The lawyer replied, "No, Your Honor, I'm just trying to get my client out of a grate situation."

# 36

## DID YOU HEAR ABOUT THE LAWYER WHO SPECIALIZES IN BEVERAGE LAW?

He's an expert in the field of "pour-torts."

## 37

# WHY DID THE LAWYER GO TO THE GYM?

He wanted to strengthen his case.

# 38

## DOCTOR, DOCTOR, I THINK I NEED A LAWYER, I CAN'T STOP SUING PEOPLE!

Well, you've certainly come to the wrong place.

# 39

## THEY SAY A GOOD LAWYER KNOWS THE LAW, BUT A GREAT LAWYER KNOWS THE JUDGE.

An even better lawyer knows where the judge hides the whiskey.

# 40

## A LAWYER NAMED SAMUEL DEWITT

Had a talent for making words fit
He'd twist and he'd bend
The truth to defend
His clients, no matter how unfit

# 41

## ISN'T IT FUNNY HOW LAWYERS ALWAYS TALK ABOUT SETTLING

But they never seem to settle down?

# 42

## AS A LAWYER, I'VE LEARNED THAT IF YOU WANT PEOPLE TO LIKE YOU

Just tell them you're an actor researching a role.

# 43

## WHY DO LAWYERS LOVE ROLLER COASTERS?

They're always looking for a good loophole.

# 44

## KNOCK, KNOCK.

Who's there?

Alpaca.

Alpaca who?

Alpaca the suitcase, you call the lawyer!

# 45

## MY LAWYER IS SO PERSUASIVE

He could convince a lion to become a vegetarian.

# 46

## WHY DID THE LAWYER BECOME A BAKER?

He loved finding ways to sweeten a deal.

# 47

## HOW MANY LAWYERS DOES IT TAKE TO CHANGE A LIGHTBULB?

Two: one to change it and one to object!

# 48

## WHY DID THE LAWYER BECOME A TAILOR?

He was great at stitching up cases.

# 49

# DOCTOR, DOCTOR, MY LAWYER CAN'T STOP LYING!

Sounds like he's suffering from a case of perjury-tis.

# 50

## I ASKED MY LAWYER IF HE WAS BUSY, AND HE SAID

"Only when I'm awake."

# 51

# A LAWYER WITHOUT A BRIEFCASE IS LIKE A FISH WITHOUT WATER

Confused and out of their element.

## 52

## HAVE YOU EVER NOTICED THAT LAWYERS AND MAGICIANS HAVE A LOT IN COMMON?

They both rely on misdirection and slight of hand.

# 53

## I ONCE KNEW A LAWYER WHO WAS SO DEDICATED TO WINNING HIS CASES THAT HE SPENT HIS FREE TIME LEARNING VENTRILOQUISM

He figured if he couldn't win with his own voice, he'd just use someone else's.

## 54

## WHY DID THE LAWYER TAKE UP YOGA?

She wanted to be more flexible in court.

# 55

## MY LAWYER IS SO RESOURCEFUL

He could find a loophole in a donut.

# 56

## WHY DID THE LAWYER BECOME A CHEF?

He had a taste for justice.

# 57

## WHAT DO YOU GET WHEN YOU CROSS A LAWYER WITH A FISH?

A shark in a suit.

## 58

## WHY DID THE BLONDE LAWYER ALWAYS CARRY A HAMMER IN HER PURSE?

She wanted to nail every case.

# 59

## THEY SAY HONESTY IS THE BEST POLICY

But my lawyer says it's also the most expensive.

# 60

## ISN'T IT FUNNY THAT A LAWYER'S FAVORITE PUNCTUATION MARK IS THE SEMICOLON?

It helps them create longer sentences.

# 61

## WHY DO LAWYERS LOVE THE BEACH?

They enjoy burying their clients in the sand.

# 62

## AN ELDERLY PATIENT NEEDED A HEART TRANSPLANT AND DISCUSSED HIS OPTIONS WITH HIS DOCTOR

The doctor presented three donors - a young athlete, a middle-aged businessman, and an attorney who practiced law for 30 years. The patient chose the attorney's heart, explaining that he wanted a heart that had not been used before.

# 63

## WHAT'S THE DIFFERENCE BETWEEN A TICK AND A LAWYER?

A tick falls off when you're dead.

# 64

## A GUY WALKED INTO A BAR AND YELLED OUT, "LAWYERS ARE ASSHOLES!"

A man in the back of the bar stood up and shouted back at him, "I take exception to that statement and I resent it greatly!" The first guy said, "Are you a lawyer?" The man responded, "No, I'm an asshole!"

# 65

## AN IT EXPERT ASKED A USER TO CHOOSE A PASSWORD OF 8 CHARACTERS.

The user replied, "Snow White and the Seven Dwarves." The IT expert commented, "I can see that you're a solicitor." The user asked how he knew, to which the IT expert replied, "The answer you gave is 100% accurate and 100% useless."

## 66

## HOW DOES AN ATTORNEY SLEEP?

First he lies on one side and then on the other.

# 67

## WHAT'S THE DIFFERENCE BETWEEN AN ACCOUNTANT AND A LAWYER?

Accountants know they're boring.

# 68

## A YOUNG LAWYER, DEFENDING A BUSINESSMAN IN A LAWSUIT

Feared he was losing the case and asked his senior partner if he should send a box of cigars to the judge to curry favor. The senior partner was horrified, but eventually, the judge ruled in the young lawyer's favor. The senior partner asked if he was glad he didn't send the cigars. The younger lawyer replied that he did send them, but he enclosed his opponent's business card with them.

# 69

## A SURGEON, AN ARCHITECT, AND A LAWYER ARE HAVING A HEATED DISCUSSION ABOUT WHICH OF THEIR PROFESSIONS IS THE OLDEST.

The surgeon argues that surgery is the oldest profession because God took a rib from Adam to create Eve. The architect claims that God was the first architect when he created the world out of chaos in seven days. The lawyer interjects, "Gentlemen, who do you think created the chaos?"

# 70

## A MAN ASKED HIS SOLICITOR, "IF I GIVE YOU $400, WILL YOU ANSWER TWO QUESTIONS FOR ME?"

The solicitor replied, "Absolutely! What's the second question?"

# 71

## A LAWYER WALKS INTO A BAR AND THE BARTENDER SAYS, "WHY THE LONG FACE?"

The lawyer replies, "I just lost my last case." The bartender says, "Well, cheer up. You still have your law degree!" The lawyer looks at him and says, "That's the problem."

# 72

## WHY DID THE LAWYER CROSS THE ROAD?

To get to the money on the other side.

# 73

## HOW DO YOU GET A GROUP OF LAWYERS TO SMILE FOR A PHOTO?

Just say, "Fees!"

# 74

## FOUR CHARACTERS ARE WALKING DOWN THE STREET - SANTA CLAUS, THE TOOTH FAIRY, AN HONEST LAWYER, AND AN OLD DRUNK.

They simultaneously spot a $20 note. Who gets it? The old drunk, of course, because the other three are fantasy creatures.

# 75

## AN ELDERLY MAN WAS TOLD BY HIS DOCTORS THAT HE DIDN'T HAVE LONG TO LIVE.

So he summoned the three most important people in his life: his doctor, his priest, and his lawyer, and said, "Today I found out I don't have long to live. So I asked you three here because you're the most important people in my life, and I need to ask a favor. Today I am going to give each of you an envelope with £50,000 in it. When I die, I would ask that all three of you throw the money in my grave." A few days later, the man passed on. The doctor said, "I have to admit I kept £10,000 of his money, he owed me lots of private medical bills. But I threw the other £40,000 in." The priest said, "I have to admit also I kept £25,000 for the church. It's all going to a good cause. And I threw the rest in." The lawyer just couldn't believe what he was hearing. "I am surprised at you two. I wrote a check for the whole amount and threw it in."

# 76

## WHY WON'T SHARKS ATTACK LAWYERS?

Professional courtesy.

# 77

## A LAWYER DIED SUDDENLY, AT THE AGE OF 45.

He got to the gates of Heaven, and the angel standing there said, "We've been waiting a long time for you." "What do you mean?" he replied, "I'm only 45, in the prime of my life. Why did I have to die now?" "45? You're not 45, you're 82," replied the angel. "Wait a minute... I'm only 45, I can show you my birth certificate." "Hold on. Let me go check," said the angel and disappeared inside. After a few minutes, the angel returned. "Sorry, but by our records, you are 82. I checked all the hours you have billed your clients, and you have to be 82..."

# 78

## WHAT IS THE DIFFERENCE BETWEEN A CATFISH AND A LAWYER?

One is a bottom-dwelling, garbage-eating scavenger. The other is a fish.

# 79

## WHY HAS THE NHS DECIDED TO USE SOLICITORS INSTEAD OF RATS FOR MEDICAL EXPERIMENTS?

There are more solicitors than rats, medical researchers aren't as attached to them, and there's nothing solicitors won't do.

# 80

## WHAT DO YOU GET WHEN YOU CROSS A LAWYER AND A JELLYFISH?

A slippery character.

# 81

## WHY DO PROGRAMMERS PREFER DOGS OVER CATS?

Because dogs have fetch API.

# 82

## WHAT DO YOU CALL A LAWYER WHO'S GONE FISHING?

A liar.

# 83

## WHY DID THE LAWYER CROSS THE ROAD?

To get to the middle.

# 84

## WHAT DO YOU CALL A LAWYER WHO IS BAD AT HIS JOB?

Your honor.

# 85

## WHAT DO YOU GET WHEN YOU CROSS A LAWYER WITH A DEMON FROM HELL?

Another lawyer.

# 86

## HOW MANY LAWYER JOKES ARE THERE?

Only three. The rest are true stories.

# 87

## WHAT DO YOU CALL A LAWYER WHO'S ALSO A CHEF?

An expert in sue-flé.

# 88

## WHAT DO YOU CALL A LAWYER GONE BAD?

A politician.

# 89

## HOW DO YOU SAVE A DROWNING LAWYER?

Take your foot off their head.

# 90

## WHAT'S THE DIFFERENCE BETWEEN A LAWYER AND A VULTURE?

Vultures can't take their wingtips off.

# 91

## WHAT DO YOU GET WHEN YOU CROSS A LAWYER WITH A WEREWOLF?

A creature that sues you for damages when it bites you.

# 92

## TWO LAWYERS WALK INTO A BAR.

The third one ducks.

# 93

## WHAT'S THE DIFFERENCE BETWEEN A CAT AND A LAWYER?

One is a ruthless, cold-blooded creature with sharp claws, and the other is just a cat.

# 94

## WHAT DO LAWYERS AND CLOUDS HAVE IN COMMON?

When they disappear, it's a beautiful day.

# 95

## WHY DID THE LAWYER CROSS THE ROAD?

To sue the chicken for trespassing.

# 96

# HOW DO YOU CONFUSE A LAWYER?

Ask them to explain their billing practices.

# 97

# KNOCK, KNOCK.

Who's there?
Heidi.
Heidi who?
Heidi evidence until the trial starts.

# 98

## WHY ARE LAWYERS SO GOOD AT SOLVING PUZZLES?

They're experts at finding loopholes.

# 99

## WHAT DO LAWYERS AND MARATHON RUNNERS HAVE IN COMMON?

They're both experts at long, drawn-out trials.

# 100

## WHY DO LAWYERS LOVE PLAYING POKER?

They're good at bluffing and raising the stakes.

Copyright © 2023 by The 100 Book Club – www.100bookclub.com

All rights reserved.

No portion of this book may be reproduced in any form without written permission from the publisher or author, except as permitted by copyright law.

Made in the USA
Monee, IL
25 September 2025

30277702R00057